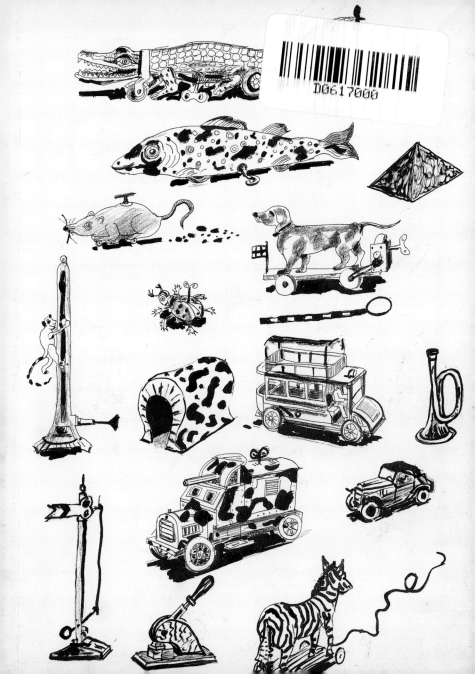

Schwitters on
the way to the
Merzbarn

I arrive in Marakeh

near perfect day

Dog's philosophy; I stink, therefore I am.

cat's philosophy ; I slink. therefore I am.

rat; I am not

The Sausage Diet

boys

drinking

eaten

albumen

King

LONDON THE SEA

ZEBEDEE

trick

last

girls

horses broth

FENCINGS

MILK

jam

MAD BIRD

leprichaun

sing, singing

Pets who care.......

fanfare for the common mug

SNAIL

lapham Junction

Half in and half out

a dog's dinner

all aboard! The Aubergine Ex

Corsicans at the Gates of ...

Fat man
Atom Bomb
Mohammed of the Black Slip

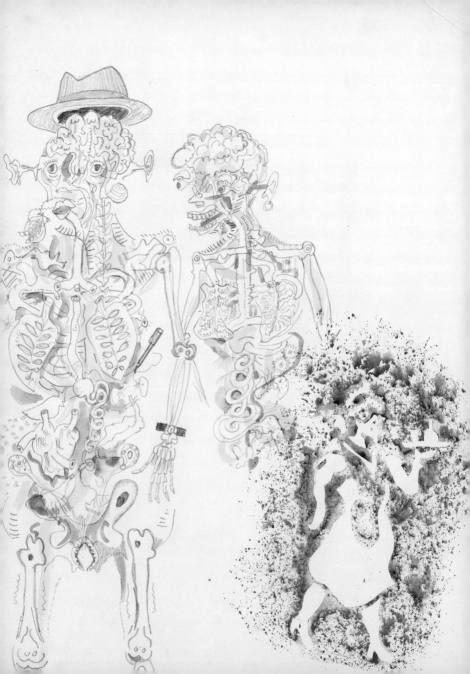

Girls Bar
Christm...

disguise

it was quite big

d'yer like my wee bogie

crickey, it's Runcorn, what's he up to?

WANTED

BEER

SPIRITS

WINE

STRONG
CURRENTS

a man of the future?

RUFUS

Rufus

the wreck of the old 97.

ntinuous warfare.

When world's collide

John Cage in a rage

MIX 'N MUD

an alternative Turner Prize

DILLO

couting for Girls

KIPPERS

NUTTY

are you a wolf or a pussycat?

Mad Dogs

Bark! and the whole world barks with you

Brass monkey

Irene Swine

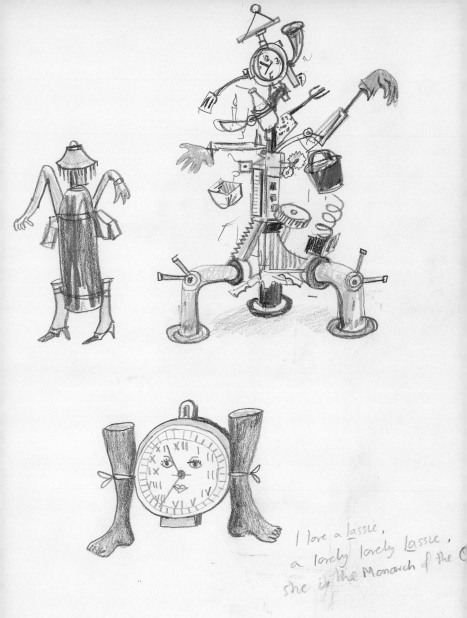

I love a lassie,
a lovely lovely lassie,
she is the Monarch of the G

The sculpture show

CIRCUS
PICCADILLY

Have the?